IN THE GARDEN

This I-SPY book belongs to: _____

Introduction

Gardening is one of Britain's most popular pastimes. A well-kept garden, no matter how big or small, can enhance the appearance of any house. There are few greater pleasures than relaxing after a hard day, among the sights, smells and sounds of a midsummer's garden on a warm evening – especially if it is a garden that you have had a hand in creating. Many gardens can be great fun to play in too – provided, of course, you don't cause any damage to the plants growing there. And gardens can be designed to encourage wildlife, or they can provide a good supply of fresh, healthy vegetables that are a delight to eat and can save the household money.

A garden may be no bigger than a window box or it may cover many hectares, as those of some of Britain's grand stately homes still do. It may be formal and ancient in style; it may imitate other gardens from all over the world, it may just be a beautifully groomed lawn or a ramble of roses or semi-wild flowers. But at a time when so much of the countryside is being gobbled up by new houses, roads, and businesses or even industrial agriculture, gardens of all shapes and sizes offer havens from the busy workaday world, a chance to be creative and provide the country as a whole with lifelines of living, breathing plants and animals.

How to use your I-SPY book

As you work through this book, you will notice that the subjects are arranged in groups which are related to the kinds of places where you are likely to find things. You need 1000 points to send off for your I-Spy certificate (see page 64) but that is not too difficult because there are masses of points in every book. As you make each I-Spy, write your score in the box and, where there is a question, double your score if you can answer it. Check your answer against the correct one on page 62.

PADDLING POOL

A paddling pool is an ideal way to cool down when the weather gets hot.

I - SPY points: 10

ROPE SWING

Rope swings are great fun. They are normally fastened to a tree. Be careful not to swing too high – and hold on tight.

I - SPY points: 15

SAND PIT

Most children would agree that no garden is complete without a sandpit. This version is neatly enclosed in to keep the sand from spreading.

I - SPY points: 10

TABLE AND CHAIRS

Garden furniture can be found in a wide variety of shapes and materials. This set comes complete with a large parasol to keep the sun off during those hot summer days!

 I - SPY points: 5

TRAMPOLINE

Some gardens have a bouncy trampoline. This is a great way to get fit and have fun at the same time.

 I - SPY points: 10

SLIDE

A garden slide can give hours of fun. How fast can you go down the slide? Be careful!

 I - SPY points: 10

BBQ

Food cooked outdoors always tastes fantastic. There are many types of barbeques available.

I - SPY points: 5

CHIMENEA

When the evening starts to get chilly, the heat from this safe fire is a great way to keep warm.

I - SPY points: 10

HAMMOCK

There is something special about snoozing in a hammock on a summers afternoon, as long as you can get in that is! How many times have you fallen out?

I - SPY points: 20

SOLAR LAMP

These solar powered lamps will light your way to the house. They only come on when it gets dark and are powered by sunlight.

 I - SPY points: 10

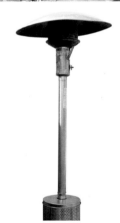

PATIO HEATER

Unfortunately, a wasteful and not very efficient way of getting warm but the rosy glow cast by a heater can help prolong that special summer evening.

 I - SPY points: 15

SWIMMING POOL

Maybe you or a friend are lucky enough to have a pool in your garden, what a great way to while away a summers day.

 I - SPY points: 20

GREENHOUSE

The glass ceiling and walls warm the inside air making an ideal place to propagate plants or germinate seeds.

What is propagating?

I - SPY points: 15,
double with answer

WOODEN SHED

All gardens need a shed. It's somewhere to store the garden tools as well as toys and bikes and of course the lawn mower.

I - SPY points: 5

DOG KENNEL

If your dog is not allowed in the house he must have one of his own! Your loyal friend deserves a cosy warm place that protects him from the weather.

I - SPY points: 50

7

GAZEBO

Most modern gazebos are temporary tent like structures made from fabric supported on poles. Long lasting wooden structures like the one in the picture may have been built for centuries.

 I - SPY points: 15

TREE HOUSE

Wouldn't it be fun to spend time playing in a house high in a tree? For most people it's just a dream but a tree house can provide hours of fun.

 I - SPY points: 30

GARAGE

What do most people keep in their garage? A car? Probably not. Garages have now become the dumping ground for toys, recycling, tools, fishing tackle and general clutter!

I - SPY points: 5

ARBOUR

Arbours are really another name for pergolas and are a type of gazebo. It's common practice to let fragrant plants such as roses ramble up the structure providing peaceful, perfumed shade for the visitor.

I - SPY points: 15

RHUBARB

This is a tall perennial plant with large wrinkly leaves and red stems which are the edible parts. Don't try to eat the leaves as they contain oxalic acid and are therefore poisonous. Its natural season is from March to July.

I - SPY points: 10

CAULIFLOWER

Cauliflowers are difficult to grow as they need a lot of rain and good soil. The white part of a cauliflower is actually just that – the flower. The proper name for it is the curd. Depending on the variety, they can be harvested between early spring and November. Some winter crops are cut between December and March.

I - SPY points: 10

BROAD BEAN

This hardy bean can be planted before winter and will burst into life in the spring. Picking usually takes place between May and August. Beware of letting the pods get too big as the beans will be too hard.

I - SPY points: 10

TOMATO

Tomatoes are easy to grow and come in many different sizes. Surprisingly not all tomatoes are red. Other colours include orange, yellow, pink, purple and green. Black or white ones are also grown! Crops are generally harvested between July – October.

I - SPY points: 5

ONION

Onions are one of the oldest vegetables and are grown in most countries of the world. They are used to flavour savoury food and can be acidic, mild and sweet or even spicy. Crops between July – September.

I - SPY points: 10

POTATO

The humble potato is our most popular vegetable and is one of the most versatile. Did you know that the average person in UK eats over 30 kilos of them every year! Early varieties, lifted in June or July are known as new potatoes, while the main crop is ready in September.

I - SPY points: 10

BRUSSEL SPROUTS

These vegetables are a type of
small cabbage and are actually
very good for you as they contain
essential vitamins and good
quantities of dietary fibre.
A useful winter crop, they crop
between August – February.

 I - SPY points: 15

BEETROOT

The red stems and the green
leaves help to brighten up the
vegetable patch. If you are not
careful your hands will be red
for days as the juice contains a
dye called betanin. They can
be pulled anytime between late
spring and autumn.

 I - SPY points: 15

MARROW

The marrow is actually a fruit
(botanically speaking) and is
part of a huge family of plants
that includes pumpkins, gherkins
and courgette. They can reach
gigantic proportions, weigh over
50kgs and reach 130cms long.
Crops between July – October.

 I - SPY points: 15

CARROTS

Easy to grow and great to eat raw or cooked, carrots are usually orange but can also be yellow, white, red or even purple! Beta-carotene in the carrot is converted into vitamin A which is necessary for good eyesight. Can be lifted late summer – October.

I - SPY points: 5

RUNNER BEANS

We eat the green pods and the multi-coloured beans in this country but in America this climbing plant is grown for its beautiful flowers. It is generally grown on frames made of bamboo and it easily grows to 2 metres high. Crops July – October.

I - SPY points: 10

PEAS

Not many things are as tasty as freshly harvested peas, just popped from its pod. They are generally served cooked but taste great raw. Early crops will be ready late May while the main crop will be ready from mid June onwards.

I - SPY points: 15

LETTUCE

Lettuce can come in six different types and is usually eaten as part of a salad. Like most vegetables it's good for us and can actually help us to sleep. Normally grown in a greenhouse, early or late in the season or in the garden in summer.

I - SPY points: 10

CABBAGE

Cabbages can be picked from the garden throughout the year. Varieties are grown throughout the world and during most seasons. They come in several shapes, which are mostly green although a red cabbage is also grown.

I - SPY points: 15

ASPARAGUS

Asparagus plants, known as crowns, have been grown around the world since the earliest times for its delicious taste and medicinal properties. We only eat the 'spears' as the young shoots are called. Crops April – June.

I - SPY points: 30

GOLDFINCH

Members of this colourful but argumentative section of the finch family are especially drawn to the bird table by tiny Niger seeds. These seeds are so small that they need to be fed using a special feeder with beak sized holes.

◯ I - SPY points: 10

GREENFINCH

These bright little finches are regulars at the peanut feeders. In winter they form quite large mixed-species feeding flocks with chaffinches and sparrows and even members of the tit family.

◯ I - SPY points: 5

SONG THRUSH

Song Thrushes are quite rare now in some places. They are a red list species, which means that they have declined as a breeding species by 50% in 25 years.

◯ I - SPY points: 20

HOUSE SPARROW

This cheeky brown bird is a regular visitor to bird tables and will often make its nest in our roof-space.

I - SPY points: 15

ROBIN

Robins sing loudest in the winter around Christmas time; it's nothing to do with the festivities, they are just staking out territories and getting ready for spring.

 I - SPY points: 5

I - SPY points: 10

STARLING

Starlings are still very common and will happily eat almost anything put out for them. In certain special roosting places they form into huge winter flocks that can be several million strong.

CHAFFINCH

The male in this image is a very colourful bird, a stark contrast to his partner who is various shades of brown. It gives her good camouflage when she is sitting on a clutch of eggs.

 I - SPY points: 5

NUTHATCH

The back of a Nuthatch is a grey-blue; their fronts the colour of a ripe conker! A quite beautiful and welcome visitor to both peanut and seed feeders. They are not nervous of people and will nest close to the house.

 I - SPY points: 20

BLUE TIT

Blue Tits are amazing acrobats. Watch carefully and you may see one hanging upside down by one leg holding a nut in the other while they eat it!

 I - SPY points: 5

GREAT SPOTTED WOODPECKER

If you are lucky you may hear them drumming on the trunk of a tree or even see one feeding at your bird table. They do however have a bad habit of breaking into nest boxes!

 I - SPY points: 15

CARRION CROW

Your chances of seeing a crow in your garden will depend on how big it is! They are very nervous and don't stay long near people. You are most likely to see them on football fields or parkland.

 I - SPY points: 15

MAGPIE

While other garden birds are in decline, Magpies are thriving and are now a common visitor to all parts of town and country.

 I - SPY points: 5

BLACKBERRY

The blackberry is also known as the bramble and it can grow into a large impenetrable bush. Please be careful of the sharp thorns when you pick the berries in late summer.

I - SPY points: 10

PEAR

Pears are closely related to apples but pear trees are usually found growing in the southern counties of Britain. Your pear will ripen faster if placed next to bananas in a fruit bowl! Trees flower in spring and bear fruit from late August – October.

 I - SPY points: 25

RASPBERRY

Raspberries bear fruit in summer or autumn dependent on variety. Quite apart from the fact that they are delicious, raspberries are also easy to grow. In fact, they can become quite wild if left unchecked.

I - SPY points: 20

I - SPY points: 10

APPLE

More than 7,500 types of apple have been cultivated and apples are grown all over the world. Fruit is ready to pick each autumn but you can save your harvest in a cold dry place like the garden shed, just check for rotten ones every few weeks.

I - SPY points: 20

PLUM

Greengages, damsons and sloes are all types of plum, but the tree in your garden will probably be a Victoria as it is the most popular of English plums. All contain a hard stone in the centre which contains the seed. If you can see white flowers on a tree in early spring it's probably a member of the plum family. Ready to pick late summer.

STRAWBERRY

Not surprisingly, strawberries are the most popular soft fruit in Britain, yet the season is very short – from mid-May to July.

 I - SPY points: 10

MICHELIN

Trees and Shrubs

ROWAN
The Rowan is a small deciduous tree that grows between 4-12 metres tall. It is easily recognised by the bunches of bright red berries that appear in early autumn and are loved by birds.

 I - SPY points: 15

LEYLAND CYPRESS
A fast growing evergreen tree that can become a nuisance. Even on poor ground it can grow to 10 metres in 10 years. It is commonly used as a hedging plant for just this reason but it needs trimming to a sensible height.

I - SPY points: 5

IVY
The common ivy is valued by homeowners as a plant to grow up unsightly fences or ugly structures. It grows quickly and provides a safe place for birds to nest and insects to hibernate.

 I - SPY points: 5

21

LILAC

The mature common Lilac is a
shrub or small tree with a main
stem diameter of about 20cms.
They only grow to about 8
metres tall and as their name
implies are covered with lilac
coloured flowers, although white
specimens can also be found.

I - SPY points: 20

BOX HEDGE

The Box is a small, sweet
smelling evergreen shrub. It has
often been used to decorate knot
gardens – the centres of which
are sometimes filled with herbs.

 I - SPY points: 15

PRIVET HEDGE

This is another common hedging
material and is related to the
Olive. It too is evergreen and
can grow tall if neglected so it
really needs to be clipped at
least twice a year. It has clumps
of tiny white flower with a distinct
aroma, which some people are
allergic to.

I - SPY points: 10

HONEYSUCKLE

This is a twining vine that rambles up and over other plants and is often found on the outside of old houses. It flowers profusely and produces the most amazing perfume on summer nights, which attracts pollinating insects.

 I - SPY points: 15

DAFFODIL

The national flower of Wales and one that we all look forward to seeing after a long dark winter. It's early flowers provide food for bumble bees and other insects emerging from hibernation.

 I - SPY points: 10

MARIGOLD

Both the French and the African varieties of this pretty yellow flower originate from Mexico. Their foliage produces a strong smell when crushed.

 I - SPY points: 10

SWEET PEA

This perfumed and colourful member of the pea family will climb to over two metres tall given support and will flower the whole summer long.

 I - SPY points: 15

 **I - SPY** points: 10

CHRYSANTHEMUM

There are hundreds of different types of chrysanthemum and their flowers are either flat and daisy-like or shaggy and round like this one. Under the right conditions they can be made to flower all year round.

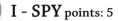 **I - SPY** points: 5

GERANIUMS

Often referred to as Geraniums, the real name of this flower is Pelargonium. One of our more common plants, they come in every colour you can think of and some even smell like mint or lemon. The plants are grown commercially; the leaves are harvested, distilled and used in the perfume industry.

TULIP

Another perennial plant and one of the most common spring flowering bulbs. The Tulip originates from Turkey and was brought to Europe in the mid-sixteenth century.

 I - SPY points: 15

PRIMROSE

Primroses are a low growing plant and by flowering so early in the year they are able to complete their life cycle before being dwarfed by taller plants.

 I - SPY points: 10

SUNFLOWER

This unmistakable, daisy-like flower will grow up to three metres high. It prefers dryish soil and, as its name suggests loves a sunny position in the garden.

 I - SPY points: 15

Flowers

SWEET WILLIAM
This short-lived perennial flower can grow up to 75cm tall, which makes it a great favourite with gardeners for the back of the border. The flowers are produced in a dense cluster and have a spicy scent. In wild plants the petals are red with a white base.

I - SPY points: 15

FUCHSIA
In some parts of the country this plant has become naturalised and makes a striking appearance in roadside hedges. It is more commonly grown in hanging baskets, ornamental pots or in ordinary flower beds.

I - SPY points: 20

CYCLAMEN
The cyclamen is a lover of cool damp shaded places. The leaves are less than 12cms high and it usually flowers in the autumn. Try looking under a spreading tree as this is a favourite place to plant then.

I - SPY points: 20

26

ASTER

We know some varieties of aster as Michaelmas daisies – so named because they flower at the time of the Michaelmas festival on 29th September.

I - SPY points: 15

DAHLIA

Originating from Mexico, Dahlias come in a wide variety of colours and provide an ideal plant for the border. It grows to about knee height and is a great favourite with flower arrangers.

I - SPY points: 10

GRAPE HYACINTH

The flower that is produced by this bulb may only be 20cm tall but what it lacks in size it makes up for in perfume!

I - SPY points: 15

SNOWDROPS

The tiny white flowers of the snowdrop herald the start of a new year in the garden. The snow may still be around but here are the first flowers of the year, nodding in the chilly breeze.

 I - SPY points: 5

WISTERIA

Clouds of flowers hang like bunches of sweet smelling grapes, all draped along the front of a house. This plant can grow up to 20 metres tall if it has a solid support.

 I - SPY points: 20

CLIMBING ROSE

These are not really climbers at all but rely on long flexible canes which need to be trained over a supporting frame, usually made of wire. They can grow to about 5 metres high and are capable of repeat flowering throughout the season.

 I - SPY points: 10

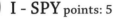

I - SPY points: 5

PANSY

Pansies are the result of successful cross breeding of several species of a wild plant; the viola. The development started in 1813 and has resulted in plants of many colours which are able to flower even during the winter.

I - SPY points: 5

ROSE

Grown for their fragrance and beautiful flowers, you are likely to find roses in most gardens. Although thought of as the 'classic' English flower, cultivated roses were developed from the Eurasian sweetbriar.

CLEMATIS

This is a large group of plants with showy flowers and a climbing habit. They like to keep their roots cool but have their heads in full sun. All the parts of the plant, while pretty, are poisonous. Take care when handling!

I - SPY points: 15

POPPIES

The corn or field poppy used to be a common sight before the age of modern weed killers. It is used to this day as a symbol of remembrance, commemorating the bravery of those who fell in the Great War 1914-1918.

I - SPY points: 10

CORNFLOWERS

Hardly seen in the wild now due to agricultural intensification, it was once a feature of every field. Luckily, we can grow it in our garden to attract and feed butterflies and bees.

I - SPY points: 15

BUDDLEIA

Also known as the butterfly bush this plant is an escape artist, having escaped from gardens it readily self-seeds into any dry ground. It will even thrive in cracks in walls. A most welcome criminal!

I - SPY points: 15

In the Shed

WHEELBARROW

The first record of a wheelbarrow is from ancient Greece around 405BC! We have been using them ever since. A typical barrow can hold 170 litres.

 I - SPY points: 10

LAWN MOWER

The first lawn mower was invented in England in 1827 and things have come a long way since then. Most are now powered by electric or small petrol engines.

 I - SPY points: 10

RIDE-ON MOWER

If you have a large garden, you may need a ride-on mower. This kind of machine makes mowing a pleasure. Some have implements such as snow ploughs or trailers attached.

I - SPY points: 15

STRING OF ONIONS

These look quite charming and rustic hanging in a shed or kitchen. Hanging them is a good way to prevent them getting damp and rotting.

I - SPY points: 15

LEAF BLOWER

This is one of those tools that makes you wonder how you ever managed without! It makes a lot of noise but saves hours of back-breaking raking.

I - SPY points: 15

SPRINKLER

A sprinkler connected to a water timer will ensure that vital water goes just to the right places at the right time.

 I - SPY points: 10

RAKE

Most seeds are tiny and they need to be sown into earth that has been broken down into small particles called a tilth. This is the tool that will remove large stones and prepare the soil.

 I - SPY points: 5

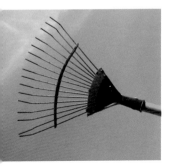

SPRING TINE RAKE

This is a versatile wide type of rake used to collect dead leaves and at the same time remove moss and other unwanted debris from a lawn.

 I - SPY points: 10

TROWEL

A standard trowel is very versatile and can be used for everything from potting on in the greenhouse to planting out in the vegetable bed. Specialist trowels are available like this one which is used just for planting bulbs.

I - SPY points: 5

HOE

Several different types of hoe have been developed each for specific purposes. This Dutch style hoe will be great for removing weeds between rows in the vegetable patch.

 I - SPY points: 5

LEAF RAKE

This is similar to the spring-tine rake but the fingers are wider which enables the rake to scoop up just the debris on top of the grass.

 I - SPY points: 5

MICHELIN

TRIMMER

Much quicker and more thorough than the old fashioned long handled shears, it's also safer as long as the correct safety equipment is worn.

 I - SPY points: 10

WATERING CAN

The fine spray is excellent for watering seedlings. On the rare occasion we have a long hot summer, this is a vital tool for the gardener.

 I - SPY points: 5

SHEARS

Shears are a very handy tool not only to keep the hedge neat and tidy but they can also cut the grass where the mower can't quite reach.

 I - SPY points: 5

SPADE

Whether your garden contains flowers, vegetables or both, at some time or other you are going to need a spade to dig the soil.

 I - SPY points: 5

FORK

The frequent gardener will appreciate a sturdy, well balanced fork. A good fork will need less effort to break the clod of earth into smaller pieces.

 I - SPY points: 5

SHOVEL

A vital tool when you need to shift large quantities of bulky material such as compost. It is not designed for digging.

 I - SPY points: 10

SECATEURS

There are different types of secateurs, each for a very specific job. This type is the most common called a bypass and they are mainly used for pruning shrubs and trees.

 I - SPY points: 10

PRUNING SAW

This saw cuts on the pulling stroke – notice that the blade is curved. Great for cutting medium sized branches, it can also be attached to an extension pole to prune high up branches.

I - SPY points: 15

DANDELION

Relied on for food by many insects that come out of hibernation early in the year, they are a weed that is hard to get rid of due to their long taproot. The young leaves can be used in salads or infused to make tea and the roots can be made into a passable coffee substitute.

 I - SPY points: 5

GROUND ELDER

Tenacious is a good word to use when describing this plant. It never gives up and will grow a whole new plant from the tiniest part left in the soil after weeding.

 I - SPY points: 5

NETTLES

Nettles are a good sign of fertile ground but they can be hard to get rid of. You can eat them when steamed or they can be turned into soup but make sure you pick them with gloves on!

I - SPY points: 5

THISTLE

The thistle has been the national emblem of Scotland since the reign of Alexander III in the 13th century.

 I - SPY points: 10

HORSETAIL

This is the only survivor of a group of plants that has been around for over 100 million years! Dinosaurs would have grazed on it and other plants of the species that reached 30 metres in height.

 I - SPY points: 10

DAISY

People who love lawns hate daisies. Most children can recognise daisies and, with a little patience, they can be made in to daisy chains.

I - SPY points: 5

I - SPY points: 5

BINDWEED

Pretty flowers maybe, but try to get rid of them and they become a nightmare. Every broken piece of root becomes a whole new plant, and they "bind" or wind themselves as they climb.

HOGWEED

There are about 60 species of Hogweed, the most common of which reaches about 1.2m but the Giant Hogweed can reach 5m! Don't touch the Giant variety if you come across it as it will give you a long lasting and painful skin rash.

I - SPY points: 10

I - SPY points: 10

BROAD-LEAVED DOCKS

Very hard to get rid of as the roots go down 1.5m into the soil. The dock is not all bad though. If you get stung by a nettle, rub a dock leaf onto the sting and you will soon forget that you were hurt.

BRAMBLE

Although Brambles scratch your skin and tear your clothes it's all worth it when the blackberry picking season arrives. Delicious when mixed with apples in a crumble or pie.

I - SPY points: 5

GOOSEGRASS

These are also known by the name of Cleavers and although rampant they are not completely useless. The roots can be made into a red dye and the mashed plant can be used to relieve poisonous bites.

I - SPY points: 10

CATERPILLAR

This is the larval form of Moths and Butterflies. Caterpillars gorge on host plants and then wrap themselves in a silk cocoon, while inside they change into the adult winged insect. Amazing!

What is the name of the process of changing from a caterpillar to a moth or butterfly?

I - SPY points: 10, double with answer

MOTH

There are thought to be over 200,000 Moth species and they come in many colours and sizes, some are poisonous. Their complex colour schemes are designed to ward off predators, mainly birds.

I - SPY points: 10

SLUGS

A slug is a gastropod without a shell; most are harmless but a few do great damage in flower borders and vegetable patches.

I - SPY points: 5

APHIDS

There are more than 500 species of Aphids which are sap-sucking insect pests. Most Aphids feed on foliage but some attack plant roots and they do untold damage to crops worldwide.

Give two other names for Aphids.

I - SPY points: 5, double with answer

SNAILS

Snails are capable of doing just as much damage as slugs. They come out at night and devour their chosen plant and then disappear before dawn into cracks in walls and under stones or logs.

I - SPY points: 5

SQUIRREL

He might look cute but this grey squirrel is really a villain. They carry a disease called squirrel pox, which is wiping out our native red squirrel as well as causing damage to large numbers of saplings.

I - SPY points: 10

SEED PACKETS

Buying a packet of seeds is a great way to start growing plants. They are normally presented in an eye catching display so you'll be sure to spot them. Choose what type you want and see the success of your hard work when the seeds start to germinate!

$\bigcirc$ **I - SPY** points: 10

SEEDLING

As a result of the gardener's patience and a little help from the weather, the seeds have finally germinated and are well on their way to becoming full sized plants.

$\bigcirc$ **I - SPY** points: 10

TROPICAL FISH

It is now quite common for garden centres to have a specialist aquarium centre. Many fish are wonderfully coloured and watching them is very relaxing. Keeping tropical fish can be difficult but the results will be well worth the hard work.

⭕ **I - SPY** points: 15

GROWBAG

Growbags are a cheap and versatile means of extending your garden. With a little knowledge and some dedication anyone can grow their own tomatoes or strawberries.

⭕ **I - SPY** points: 10

COMPOST

Compost has been made commercially for years and is sold in tough plastic sacks. Peat-free compost is better from an environmental standpoint as harvesting peat damages that delicate environment.

⭕ **I - SPY** points: 10

CHICKEN

Not quite visitors and not quite pets! Looking after your own small flock is a very rewarding pastime and of course you get fresh eggs every day.

 I - SPY points: 10

BADGER

We tend to think that badgers are woodland animals, living in setts in the countryside. They easily adapt to urban life and colonies have been found in Surrey, Sussex and Yorkshire to name a few.

 I - SPY points: 35

DOG

Most dogs are happy to play in the garden with just the slightest encouragement.

 I - SPY points: 5

CAT

For most of the day (and most of the night) most cats are asleep but when they wake up they become like tigers, hunting prey in the garden just like a wild animal.

 I - SPY points: 5

FOX

This is a real wild animal! Foxes are known for their cunning and have colonised some towns completely, helped by some people feeding them on a regular basis.

 I - SPY points: 20

GUINEA PIG

They make great pets and they appear to enjoy being let out on the lawn to sunbathe, socialise and eat some fresh grass.

 I - SPY points: 10

LADYBIRD

Ladybirds are voracious predator and definitely the gardener's friend as they eat scale insects and aphids. There is no truth in the myth that the more spots, the older the insect!

I - SPY points: 10

BEETLE

There are over 300,000 species of beetles and they have been on earth for at least 300 million years. In that time they have colonised every type of habitat, some even live on and under water.

I - SPY points: 10

HONEY BEE

Without the humble honey bee our cupboards, fridges and freezers would be half empty! We often don't appreciate what vital job bees do with the pollination of flowers, especially those of fruit trees and shrubs.

I - SPY points: 10

SPIDER

In spite of what you may think, spiders are doing us all a favour! Their webs catch all sorts of insects which the spider then eats. Without them our gardens and houses would be overrun with insect pests.

I - SPY points: 5

PEACOCK BUTTERFLY

Due to our changing climate, peacocks are waking up from hibernation earlier every year so look for them in late March or early April. They are one of the longest living butterflies and some may survive almost a whole year.

I - SPY points: 20

RED ADMIRAL

Another beauty, this large butterfly is often seen in your garden in almost any month of the year particularly if you have a butterfly bush or ivy.

I - SPY points: 20

SLOW WORM

These are not worms or snakes at all but legless lizards. They can grow to 50cms long and live as long as 30 years. They are truly a gardener's friend as they eat slugs.

 I - SPY points: 20

HEDGEHOG

If you go to the backdoor to call in your cat for the night, you may well hear something snuffling in the flower beds. Don't be alarmed, it's not a giant beast just a hungry hedgehog looking for snails and slugs.

 I - SPY points: 15

WORM

Earthworms are the unseen heroes of the garden. They recycle dead leaves, excavate tunnels which aerate the soil and at the same time help with drainage. All these activities benefit our flowers, vegetables and trees.

 I - SPY points: 5

BEE HIVE

It's not usually a problem having a colony of bees in your garden as unlike wasps, they are after the pollen and nectar from flowers and not your sandwiches or fizzy drinks.

I - SPY points: 15

BIRD BATH

Not only do birds need fresh clean water to drink, they also need it to bathe. It's absolutely vital that they keep their feathers clean. A nice clean, shallow bath quite close to some bushes where they can hide and preen will be just perfect.

I - SPY points: 10

BONSAI

This is the ancient far-eastern practice of growing miniaturised trees in containers. The plants are fussed over by their owner who constantly monitors every aspect of their life. These trees can be hundreds of years old and cost hundreds of pounds!

I - SPY points: 20

BIRD TABLE

Having a table near to a window will enable you to watch birds in comfort. Keep feeding them all year and the birds will repay your kindness and dedication by helping to keep insect pests away from your plants.

I - SPY points: 10

STONE WALLING

Using stone to form a boundary wall is a practise that has gone on for thousands of years. This type of wall provides numerous nooks and crannies for plants to grow and insects to hide in.

 I - SPY points: 10

POND

With a pond in the garden you will be able to spot all types of creatures arriving for a drink or a bath. It doesn't have to be large, all standing water is appreciated by nature, just remember to remove the fallen leaves in autumn and keep it topped up.

I - SPY points: 10

DECKING

Wooden decking is often raised up above the level of the lawn and is a very relaxing place to sit and enjoy the garden.

I - SPY points: 5

GRAVEL DRIVE

As long as you are prepared to weed occasionally, gravel looks very smart, natural and even sounds nice and scrunchy!

 I - SPY points: 15

FOUNTAIN

The sound of water falling from a fountain into a pool is very relaxing and reminds us of a family day out, sitting on a river bank fishing or maybe having a family picnic.

 I - SPY points: 10

STATUE

Statues tend to be carved from blocks of stone or cast metal of which bronze is the most common. The subject can vary from animals to mythical figures. They are often used to provide a focal point in the garden.

 I - SPY points: 10

FENCING

Fences are used to create a boundary between properties or just create definition between different areas of the same garden. They are made of iron or wood and can be quite decorative.

 I - SPY points: 5

UNUSUAL CONTAINER

A quaint and pretty way to recycle your old boots when they wear out or just start to leak! Make sure that they do have a few holes in the sole for drainage or your plants will drown.

 I - SPY points: 5

PLANT CONTAINER

What better way to show off a valued and beautiful flowering plant than by using a contrasting coloured container. They can be made of plastic or pottery and are available in a wide variety of shapes and colours.

I - SPY points: 5

CACTUS

Cactus plants are not as hard to grow as is thought, and it's not true that they only flower every seven years! Most of the time they are kept indoors but during dry weather there is no reason why they can't be outside in the sun and fresh air.

I - SPY points: 15

FLOWER POTS

The can be made of high density plastic or terracotta which is a type of pottery. The most common types vary in size from 5cm to 30cm diameter. Special giant black ones are available which can hold 500 litres of compost.

I - SPY points: 5

WATER WELL

Most modern water wells are just for ornamental purposes and contain very little water. Quite often you can throw money into large water wells to make a wish come true.

 I - SPY points: 15

GARDEN GNOME

Garden gnomes were first made by a German potter in response to a local myth about a gnome's willingness to help in the garden at night. They were introduced to England in 1847 and are still popular today.

I - SPY points: 15

PARASOL

A perfect way to keep cool on a hot day. It will also offer some protection from the sun and help in keeping your food and drinks cool.

 I - SPY points: 15

HOME-MADE COMPOST

These inexpensive plastic bins can be sited away from the house and blend well with surrounding foliage. Just keep topping it up with kitchen peelings, some hedge clippings and a little grass and very soon you will have your own home-made compost.

 I - SPY points: 10

RECYCLING BIN

These special bins are provided by the local councils to help us recycle all sorts of different materials. Check carefully, they are not all green and they are not all this shape.

 I - SPY points: 5

WATER BUTT

Rainwater is collected from the roof of your house using gutters and pipes and is better for your plants than tap water. If your house is fitted with a water meter, a butt will save money too!

 I - SPY points: 10

WATER LILIES

Water lilies are actually plants that have their roots in mud at the bottom of the pond and their flowers and leaves up on the surface. The flowers are often white or pink.

 I - SPY points: 10

TOAD

The common toad is mostly nocturnal and hides in sheltered places during the day. They are broad and squat with warty skin. To deter predators, they secrete an irritant from their skin.

 I - SPY points: 15

FROG SPAWN

Frogs are getting much rarer so if you see frog spawn leave it in the pond and watch to see it hatch into tadpoles and then into froglets.

I - SPY points: 15

HERE ARE SOME RECOMMENDED GARDENS TO VISIT

15 points for each garden visited, 10 points if you visit one not on the list

RHS GARDEN HARLOW CARR
Crag Lane, Harrogate, North Yorkshire, HG3 1QB, Tel: 01423 565418

RHS GARDEN ROSEMOOR
Great Torrington, Devon, EX38 8PH, Tel: 01805 624067

RHS GARDEN HYDE HALL
Westerns Approach, Rettendon, Chelmsford, Essex, CM3 8ET, Tel: 01245 400256

RHS GARDEN WISLEY
Woking, Surrey, GU23 6QB, Tel: 08452 609000

SCOTLAND

ABRIACHAN GARDENS
Loch Ness Side, by Inverness, IV3 8LA Tel: 01463 861232, www.lochnessgarden.com

DRUMMOND GARDENS
Muthill, Crieff, Perth and Kinross, PH7 4HZ Tel: 01764 681433 www.drummondcastlegardens.co.uk

DUNDEE UNIVERSITY BOTANIC GARDEN
Riverside Drive, Dundee, DD2 1QH Tel: 01382 381190, www.dundee.ac.uk/botanic

DUNROBIN CASTLE GARDENS
Golspie, Sutherland, KW10 6SF Tel: 01408 633177, www.dunrobincastle.co.uk

FLOORS CASTLE GARDENS
Kelso, Roxburghshire, TD5 7SF Tel: 01573 223333, www.floorscastle.com

GEILSTON GARDEN
(National Trust for Scotland) Main Road, Cardross, Dumbarton, G82 5HD, Tel: 08444 932219, www.nts.org.uk

GLENWHAN GARDEN
Dunragit, by Stranraer, Wigtownshire, DG9 8PH, Tel: 01581 400222, www.glenwhangardens.co.uk

INWOOD GARDEN
Carberry, near Musselburgh, East Lothian, EH21 8PZ, Tel: 01316 654550, www.inwoodgarden.com

LEITH HALL, GARDEN & ESTATE
(National Trust for Scotland) Huntly, Aberdeenshire, AB54 4NQ Tel: 08444 932164, www.nts.org.uk

THREAVE GARDEN AND ESTATE
(National Trust for Scotland) Castle Douglas, Dumfries and Galloway, DG7 1RX, Tel: 08444 932245, www.nts.org.uk

TOROSAY CASTLE AND GARDENS
Torosay Castle, Craignure, Isle of Mull, PA65 6AY, Tel: 01680 812421, www.torosay.com

NORTH WEST

ARLEY HALL AND GARDENS
Arley, Northwich, Cheshire, CW9 6NA Tel: 01565 777353, www.arleyhallandgardens.com

DALEMAIN HISTORIC HOUSE AND GARDENS
Dalemain, Penrith, Cumbria, CA11 0HB Tel: 01768 4 86450, www.dalemain.com

HOLKER HALL AND GARDENS
Cark-in-Cartmel, nr Grange-over-Sands,
Cumbria LA11 7PL, Tel: 01539 558328,
www.holker-hall.co.uk

NORTH EAST

THE ALNWICK GARDEN
Denwick Lane, Alnwick, Northumberland, NE66
1YU, Tel: 01665 511350,
www.alnwickgarden.com

NORMANBY HALL COUNTRY PARK
Normanby, Scunthorpe, North Lincolnshire,
DN15 9HU, Tel: 01724 720588

RABY CASTLE
Staindrop, Darlington, Co. Durham, DL2 3AH
Tel: 01833 660202, www.rabycastle.com

SCAMPSTON HALL WALLED GARDEN
Malton, North Yorkshire, YO17 8NG
Tel: 01944 759111, www.scampston.co.uk

THORP PERROW ARBORETUM AND
WOODLAND GARDEN
Bedale, North Yorkshire, DL8 2PR
Tel: 01677 425323, www.thorpperrow.com

WENTWORTH CASTLE GARDENS
Lowe Lane, Stainborough, Barnsley, South
Yorkshire, S75 3ET, Tel: 01226 776040

EAST ANGLIA

ANGLESEY ABBEY GARDENS
Quy Road, Lode, Cambridge, Cambridgeshire,
CB25 9EJ, Tel: 01223 810080
www.nationaltrust.org.uk/angleseyabbey

THE BETH CHATTO GARDENS
Elmstead Market, Colchester, Essex, CO7 7DB
Tel: 01206 822007, www.bethchatto.co.uk

EAST RUSTON OLD VICARAGE
East Ruston, Norwich, Norfolk, NR12 9HN
Tel: 01692 650432,
www.e-rustonoldvicaragegardens.co.uk

GRIMSTHORPE CASTLE
Bourne, Lincolnshire, PE10 0LY
Tel: 01778 591205, www.grimsthorpe.co.uk

HOUGHTON HALL
Estate Office, Houghton Hall, King's Lynn,
Norfolk, PE31 6UE, Tel: 01485 528569
www.houghtonhall.com

WYKEN HALL
Stanton, Bury St Edmunds, Suffolk, IP31 2DW
Tel: 01359 250262,
www.wykenvineyards.co.uk

SOUTH EAST

BEDGEBURY
Bedgebury National Pinetum, Goudhurst, Kent,
TN17 2SL, Tel: 01580 879820
www.forestry.gov.uk/bedgebury

BENINGTON LORDSHIP
Stevenage, Hertfordshire, SG2 7BS
Tel: 08701 261709,
www.beningtonlordship.co.uk

BLENHEIM PALACE, PARK AND GARDENS
Woodstock, Oxfordshire, OX20 1PX
Tel: 01993 811091, www.blenheimpalace.com

BORDE HILL GARDEN
Balcombe Road, Haywards Heath, West
Sussex, RH16 1XP, Tel: 01444 450326,
www.bordehill.co.uk

ENGLEFIELD HOUSE
Reading, Berkshire, RG7 5EN,
Tel: 01189 302221,
www.englefieldestate.co.uk

EXBURY GARDENS
Exbury, Southampton, SO45 1AZ
Tel: 02380 891203, www.exbury.co.uk

GOODNESTONE PARK GARDENS
Goodnestone Park, nr Wingham, Canterbury,
Kent, CT3 1PL, Tel 01304 840107,
www.goodnestoneparkgardens.co.uk

SOUTH WEST

ABBOTSBURY SUBTROPICAL GARDENS
Abbotsbury, Weymouth, DT3 4LA
Tel: 01305 871387,
www.abbotsburyplantsales.co.uk

BROADLEAS GARDENS
Broadleas, Devizes, Wiltshire, SN10 5JQ
Tel: 01380 722035

MARWOOD HILL GARDEN
Barnstaple, North Devon, EX31 4EB
Tel: 01271 342528,
www.marwoodhillgarden.co.uk

TAPELEY PARK
Instow, nr Bideford, North Devon, EX39 4NT
Tel: 01271 342558/01271 860597

TREBAH GARDEN
Mawnan Smith, nr Falmouth, Cornwall, TR11
5JZ, Tel: 01326 252200,
www.trebah-garden.co.uk

CENTRAL

ARLEY ARBORETUM AND GARDENS
Upper Arley, nr Bewdley, Worcestershire DY12
1XG, Tel: 01299 861368/868,
www.arley-arboretum.org.uk

BLUEBELL ARBORETUM AND NURSERY
Annwell Lane, Smisby, Ashby-de-la Zouch,
South Derbyshire, LE65 2TA

Tel: 01530 413700,
www.bluebellnursery.co.uk

GARDEN ORGANIC RYTON
Ryton-on-Dunsmore, Coventry, CV8 3LG
Tel: 02476 303517,
www.gardenorganic.org.uk

WESTONBIRT
The National Arboretum, Westonbirt, Tetbury,
Gloucestershire, GL8 8QS, Tel: 01666
880220, www.forestry.gov.uk/westonbirt

WALES

CAE HIR
Gerddi Cae Hir Gardens, Cribyn, Lampeter,
Ceredigion SA48 7NG, Tel: 01570 470839,
www.caehirgardens.ws

DYFFRYN GARDENS AND ARBORETUM
St. Nicholas, Vale of Glamorgan, CF5 6SU
Tel: 02920 593328,
www.dyffryngardens.org.uk

THE NATIONAL BOTANIC GARDEN OF WALES
Carmarthenshire, SA32 8HG
Tel: 01558 668768,
www.gardenofwales.org.uk

PICTON CASTLE AND WOODLAND GARDENS
Haverfordwest, Pembrokeshire, SA62 4AS
Tel: 01437 751326, www.pictoncastle.co.uk

PLAS BRONDANW GARDENS
Llanfrothen, Penrhyndeudraeth,
Gwynedd, LL48 6SW, Tel: 01743 241181

Index

First published by Michelin Maps and Guides 2010
© Michelin, Proprietaires-Editeurs 2010.
Michelin and the Michelin Man are registered
Trademarks of Michelin.
Created and produced by Blue Sky Publishing Limited.
All rights reserved. No part of this publication may be
reproduced, copied or transmitted in any form without the
prior consent of the publisher.
Ragworms are often used by fishermen as they make ideal
fish bait. They are found in muddy or gravely conditions.
The publisher gratefully acknowledges the contribution of
the I-Spy team: Camilla Lovell, Graeme Newton-Cox and
Ruth Neilson in the production of this title.
The publisher gratefully acknowledges the contribution
and assistance from all the sites, people and images used
in the book, with special thanks to The Royal Horticultural
Society. The publisher gratefully acknowledges the
contribution of David Fenwick, Joel Veitch and Unitaw
Limited who provided the photographs in this book. Other
images in the public domain and used under a creative
commons license.
Reprinted 2013   16 15 14 13 12 11 10 9 8

HOW TO GET YOUR I-SPY **CERTIFICATE** AND **BADGE**

Every time you score 1000 points or more in an I-Spy book, you can apply for a certificate

Here's what to do, step by step:

Certificate

- Ask an adult to check your score
- Ask his or her permission to apply for a certificate
- Apply online to www.ispymichelin.com
- Enter your name and address and the completed title
- We will send you back via e mail your certificate for the title

Badge

- Each I-Spy title has a cut out (page corner) token at the back of the book
- Collect five tokens from different I-Spy titles
- Put Second Class Stamps on two strong envelopes
- Write your own address on one envelope and put a £1 coin inside it (for protection). Fold, but do not seal the envelope, and place it inside the second envelope
- Write the following address on the second envelope, seal it carefully and post to:

I-Spy Books
Michelin Maps and Guides
Hannay House
39 Clarendon Road
Watford
WD17 1JA

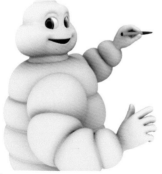